LOVE SONGS OF THE IRISH

Love Songs of the Irish

COLLECTED AND ANNOTATED BY

JAMES N. HEALY

MUSIC WRITTEN OUT BY

CON O'DONOVAN

with chords suitable for guitar, piano and organ

THE MERCIER PRESS
DUBLIN AND CORK

15224

The Mercier Press Ltd
4 Bridge Street Cork
25 Lower Abbey Street, Dublin 1

ISBN 0 85342 497 7

To my friend
John B. Keane
of Listowel
With whom I have
soldiered, and sung songs
over the past 18 years.

ACKNOWLEDGEMENTS

The author and publisher would like to thank all those who gave permission to use the copyright material in this book.

PREFACE

> I have loved you, oh mildest and fairest,
>> With love that could scarce be more warm —
> I have loved you, oh brightest and rarest,
>> Not less for your mind than your form.
> I've adored you since ever I met you,
>> O, Rose without briar or stain,
> And if e'er I forsake or forget you
>> Let Love be ne'er trusted again.

The above song is a translation by James Clarence Mangan of an Irish song to the air now known to us as *'An Cailín Deas Crúite na mBó' ('The Pretty Dairy-Maid').* There are a number of translations from the original Irish lyric—the best of these is probably George Sigerson's Verses commencing *'The Gold Rain of Eve was descending'*, but the above is from an original Irish song to the air by *An Mangaire Súgach (The Merry Pedler)*, Aindrias MacCraith, an eccentric gentleman who was one of the poets of the river Maigue in County Limerick. It proves in fact, if proof is needed, that since MacCraith died in 1793, the air is probably older than any of the words we know to it in either language. It was first set down by Edward Bunting, who had been engaged to take down for posterity the tunes played by a number of old harpists brought together in Belfast in 1792 so that the old melodies would be preserved. For young Bunting it was the beginning of a lifetime spent on the preservation of Irish music. Of course Irish tunes had been included in printed books before his time, but mainly as incidental to English collections, and a collection of Bunting's first volume of 56 tunes (of which *An Cailín Deas Crúite na mBó* was the fifty-fourth) was the earliest systematic effort to get them down on manuscript before the tunes died with the fingers of the harpers who played them. Later he would be criticised for simplifying the airs and taking them down without the extravagant embellishments of which the traditional musicians were so fond; but with so much to do, and in so short a time; and having probably to deal with aged harpers, cranky when pressed for repetition, he did very well. His collections were a basis for a great surge of lyric writing in English to old Irish tunes which became a notable fashion of the nineteenth century.

Thomas Moore, despite detractors, could probably be considered the most eminent in the field: he would be harshly treated after his time for bastardising the music and turning it into soppy songs for Drawing-Room matrons and maidens. This charge could not be entirely denied but it is fair to comment that, among other sources, Moore took much of his music note for note from Bunting, and on the basis that a man must be judged on his best work, some of his numbers are superb. There were Anglo-Irish lyric writers to old Irish tunes before Moore's time; and there would be many later who would utilise old tunes or write original music, but it was Moore who brought the appreciation of Irish music, even in his changed form, to a larger audience.

One of the important features of the last century, however, were the writers who made direct translations from the known songs written in the Irish language. There was a great wealth of these songs, but during the eighteenth century the language was being eroded almost out of existence by the operation of savage Penal Laws which were visited on the people following Irish support for the Jacobite cause, and had the purpose of eliminating the Gaelic way of life. Songs were still being written in Irish — many indeed in support of the Jacobites — but the old Bards such as Carolan who travelled the country from the hospitality of one big house to another, and were represented by those harpers assembled in Belfast, had diminished in numbers by the end of the century. When the nineteenth century dawned their representatives would be such as the poet, Patrick O'Kelly, addressing his flowery compliments in

6

English: a tattered remnant of what the old bards had been. There would still be in the *Hidden Ireland* of which Daniel Corkery wrote such as Eoghan Ruadh Ó Súilleabháin, some-time schoolmaster but more often wandering *spailpín* and sailor; and Aindrias MacCraith in Croom by the Maigue: but the great bulk of the songs in Gaelic, from this time or before, came from writers whose names we do not know, and often in versions which varied from Province to Province. They formed the origin of some of the most beautiful Love Songs in this or any other language, and it is the derivations from these songs, with the added treasure of songs in the English language, which give the basis for this book.

Love they say is a universal language, but it has always been aided by the gift of song. The Irish, though preoccupied by their sadnesses and travails, never forgot the rogueries, the sighing and the necessary flattery that went with the art of loving—and they sang about it. I hope this volume will help you to sing too; and maybe to be successful in the quest for that ideal lady, or gentleman, of your heart. There are some songs which I would like to have included—but was unable for copyright reasons.

I have done my best to make all acknowledgements; if any have been inadvertently omitted I can only apologise.

James N. Healy

CONTENTS

LOVE SONGS OF THE IRISH

Most of the collections of Irish lyrics which have been made over the last hundred and fifty years have included our first two numbers.

They were written by a lady, a gentlewoman, and that fact alone would have been enough to have them labelled 'drawing room' ballads with some scorn by some of the more politically-minded lyric writers of the middle of the last century; but the fact remains that they are good lyrics matched to suitable tunes, and as sentimental Irish love songs they stand on their own feet. John McCormack made a particular success of both of them. The music to the first was written by a gentleman named Barker specially for the song, but the second, in the more usual practice of the time, used an old Gaelic tune, *An Cailín Deas Crúite na mBó (The Pretty Dairy-Maid)* a pastoral song which has had a number of translations. One doubts whether any of these translations have the tenderness of *Terence's Farewell*. The lady lyricisit was born Helen Selina Sheridan (1807-1867), a granddaughter of Richard Brinsley Sheridan. She became Lady Dufferin, and later again, in a second marriage late in life, the Countess of Gifford.

1. LAMENT OF THE IRISH EMIGRANT

Words: Helen, Lady Dufferin
Music: G. Barker

ANDANTE

I'M SIT-TING BY THE STILE MA-RY WHERE WE SAT SIDE BY SIDE- ON A

BRIGHT MAY MOR-NING LONG A-GO WHEN FIRST YOU WERE MY BRIDE, THE

11

CORN WAS SPRING-ING FRESH AND GREEN AND THE LARK SANG LOUD AND HIGH, AND THE RED WAS ON YOUR LIPS MA-RY AND THE LOVE LIGHT IN YOUR EYE — , THE PLACE IS LIT-TLE CHANGED MA-RY THE DAY IS BRIGHT AS THEN — , THE LARK'S LOUD SONG IS IN MY EAR AND THE CORN IS GREEN A-GAIN — , BUT I MISS THE SOFT CLASP OF YOUR HAND AND THE BREATH WARM ON YOUR CHEEK, AND I STILL KEEP LIST'-NING TO THE WORDS YOU NE-VER MORE MAY SPEAK — , YOU NE-VER MORE MAY SPEAK — .

I'm very lonely now, Mary
For the poor make no new friends;
But, Oh we love the better still
The few Our Father sends;
And you were all I had, Mary,
My blessing and my pride;
There's nothing left to care for now,
Since my poor Mary died.

I'm bidding you a long farewell,
My Mary kind and true,
But I'll not forget you, darling,
In the land I'm going to;
They say: 'There's bread and work for all,
And the sun shines always there',
But I'll not forget old Ireland;
Were it fifty times as fair.

12

2. TERENCE'S FAREWELL

Words: Helen, Lady Dufferin
Air: An Cailín Deas Crúite na mBó
(The Pretty Dairy-Maid)

Och, those English, deceivers by nature,
    Though maybe you'd think them sincere,
They'll say you're a sweet, charming creature,
    But don't you believe them, my dear.
O, Kathleen, agrah! don't be minding
    The flattering speeches they make;
But tell them a poor lad in Ireland
    Is breaking his heart for your sake.

It's folly to keep you from going,
    Though, faith, it's a mighty hard case,
For, Kathleen, you know there's no knowin'
    When next I shall see your sweet face.
And when you come back to me, Kathleen,
    None the better will I be off then;
You'll be spakin' such beautiful English,
    Sure I won't know my Kathleen again.

13

Eh, now, where's the need of this hurry?
Don't fluster me so in this way!
I forgot 'twixt the grief and the flurry,
Every word I was maynin' to say.
Now just wait a minute, I bid ye;
Can I talk if you bother me so?
Och, Kathleen, my blessing go with ye,
Every inch of the way that you go.

The air was preserved by Bunting in his first collection in 1796 (No. 54). Since it appears in slightly different form in other collections (such as Holdens *Old Established Irish Tunes 1806*, and as *Douchig for Sport* in a collection of pipe music by O'Farrell (1796) it was obviously known for some time before our earliest record of it.

The form of pastoral song presented by *An Cailín Deas Crúite na mBó* was a favourite theme for song writers in Irish, and later for their rustic counterparts writing in English. A gentleman is strolling through the fields ('As I walked out one morning, I saw a maiden fair') when he sees a beautiful girl, and immediately begins to pay flowery compliments to her. One of the best known, in words and air, was *Fáinne Geal an Lae (The Dawning of the Day)*.

3. THE DAWNING OF THE DAY

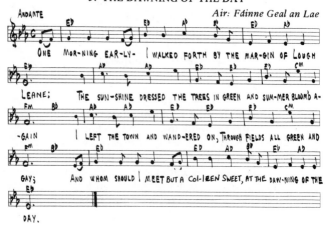

14

No cap or cloak this maiden wore, her neck and feet were
[bare;
Down to the grass in ringlets fell her glossy golden hair;
A milking pail was in her hand, she was lovely young and gay;
She bore the palm from Venus bright, by the dawning of
[the day.

On a mossy bank I sat me down, with the maiden by my side;
With gentle words I courted her, and asked her to be my
[bride;
She said, 'Young man don't bring me blame,' and swiftly
[turned away;
And the morning light was shining bright, at the dawning of
[the day.

There were formerly a number of airs used for this Irish
song, but the one above, often now utlised in march form
by bands, is today widely accepted. There are many other
examples of this kind of lyric such as *The Irish Girl, The
Cottage Maid, The Colleen Rua, The Angler, One Evening
Fair.*

The Dawning of the Day is only one of the wealth of
songs which has come to us from the rich pool of Gaelic
origin. There are very few which have definitive versions —
for a translation from any language is in itself a new work
which must stand on its own feet. This applies more to
poetry than to prose, and it applies particularly when translating from Irish to English, because of the difference in the
systems of metre, rhythm and rhyme. English verse, particularly up to modern times, depended very much on the
words at the end of lines having a rhyming sound with one
another; the Gaelic method, developed through the Bardic
schools of generations, depended more on vowel sounds
and subtle internal rhythms. J. J. Callanan in the early nineteenth century was one of the earliest poets to endeavour
to reproduce the Irish form when turning such old songs as
Cluain Meala and *The Outlaw of Loch Leane* into English.
When the fashion developed later in his century some of the
more favoured old songs attracted a number of translators.

Some produced entirely different versions of the same songs; and the original Irish lyric was occasionally ignored. Now follows a very beautiful Jacobite song which has come down to us with a number of different tunes. In its earliest English form it is a lament by a young maiden for her 'Wild Goose' who has gone to fight on the Continent. This uses one of the tunes most familiar to me. Gavan Duffy wrote of 'the inexpressible tenderness of the air and the deep feeling and simplicity of the words.'

4. SHULE AROON

Words: Trad.
Air: Siubhail a Rún

His hair was black, his eye was blue,
His arm was stout, his word was true.
I wish in my heart I was with you,
Is go-de-thu, Avourneen slaun, etc.

'Tis oft I sat on my true love's knee,
Many a fond story he told to me,
He told me things that ne'er shall be
Is go-de-thu, Avourneen slaun, etc.

I sold my rock, I sold my reel;
When my flax was spun I sold my wheel
To buy my love a sword of steel,
Is go-de-thu, Avourneen slaun, etc.

16

But when King James was forced to flee,
The Wild Geese spread their wings to sea,
And bore my bouchal far from me,
Is go-de-thu, Avourneen slaun, etc.

I saw them sail from Brandon Hill,
Then down I sat and cried my fill,
That every tear would turn a mill,
Is go-de-thu, Avourneen slaun, etc.

I wish the King would return to reign,
And bring my true love back again;
I wish, and wish, but I wish in vain,
Is go-de-thu, Avourneen slaun, etc.

I'll dye my petticoat, I'll dye it red,
And round the world I'll beg my bread,
Till I find my love, alive or dead,
Is go-de-thu, Avourneen slaun, etc.

The following is a free translation of the meaning of the chorus:

Come, come, oh come, my love;
Come to me quickly and gently move,
Walk through the door and fly with me
And a blessing walk with you, Machree.

The close connection between Scottish and Irish Jacobites and the common sharing of many songs can be noted from the old Scottish song preserved in David Herd's *Scottish Songs*, vol. II, 1776:

I'd sell my rock, my reel, my tow
My guide grey mare and hacket cow
To buy my love a tartan plaid,
Because he is a roving blade.

The argument will go on for a long time as to whether the origin of many of the airs involved was Scottish or Irish. To be truthful we do not know; and it would be very difficult to be dogmatic about more than one or two of the disputed tunes. Sufficient to say that the last time these two great Gaelic nations showed a common purpose was for the lost cause of 'Bonnie Prince Charlie' during 'the '45'.

The second version given here has words which have no connection (apart from the chorus) with the original. This method might be scorned by the most fervent traditionalists (I have heard them) but it cannot be denied that Griffin's verses made a simple and delightful love song. It was the second most familiar air. Both songs are very beautiful, each in its own way.

5. MY MARY OF THE CURLING HAIR

Words: Gerald Griffin
Air: Siubhail a Rún (Second Air)

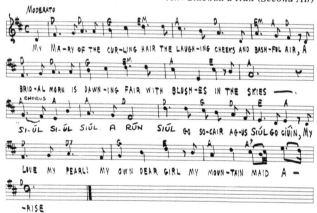

For we were known from infancy,
    Thy father's hearth was home to me.
No selfish love was mine for thee,
    Unholy and unwise.
    Chorus:

I am no stranger proud and gay
    To win thee from thy home away,
And find thee for a distant day
    A theme for wasting sighs.
    Chorus:

But soon my love shall be my bride,
And happy by our own fireside
My veins shall feel the rosy tide
Which lingering hope denies.
Chorus:

Gerald Griffin (b. Limerick 1803 – d. Cork 1840) was a novelist and poet whose most noted work was a novel, *The Collegians*, very famous in its time. He wrote it as a young journalist after he had attended the trial of John Scanlon, the murderer of Ellie Hanley (*The Colleen Bawn*) at Limerick in 1820. His story was based on these characters and Boucicault later wrote a play on the novel transferring the locale to Killarney. Later Benedict added the Ballad Opera *The Lily of Killarney*. Even today jarveys in Killarney will point out 'The Colleen Bawn Rock' to unsuspecting tourists. Maybe they believe it. The murder in fact took place on the Shannon near Glin.

Griffin went to London but later abandoned his writing career to become a Christian Brother. He died in Cork of typhus and is buried there in the grounds of the North Monastery.

Very few of these translated songs can be said to have a definitive translation, as has already been remarked. The one that follows is an exception. It is the work of Doctor George Petrie (Dublin, 1798-1866), distinguished scholar, artist and antiquarian; a skilled musician and one of the most important researchers in the field of Irish music.

6. THE SNOWY-BREASTED PEARL

Words: Translated from the Irish by George Petrie
Air: Péarla an bhrollaigh bháin
(The Pearl of the White Breast)

THERE'S A COL-LEEN FAIR AS MAY, FOR A YEAR AND FOR A' DAY I HAVE SOUGHT BY EV'RY WAY HER HEART TO GAIN —. THERE'S NO ART OF TONGUE OR EYE, FOND

YOUTHS WITH MAIDENS TRY, BUT I'VE TRIED WITH CEASE-LESS SIGH, YET TRIED IN VAIN———. IF TO FAR OFF FRANCE OR SPAIN SHE CROSSED THE RAG-ING MAIN, HER FACE TO SEE A-GAIN, THE SEAS I'D BRAVE———. BUT IF 'TIS HEAV'N'S DE-CREE, THAT MINE SHE MAY NOT BE, MAY THE SON OF MA-RY ME IN MER-CY SAVE———.

Oh, thou blooming milk-white dove
To whom I've given my love,
Do not ever thus reprove
        My constancy.

There are maidens would be mine,
With wealth in the land and kine,
If my heart would but incline
        To turn from thee.

But a kiss with welcome bland
And touch of thy fair hand,
Is all that I demand,
        Would'st thou not spurn.

For if not mine, dear girl,
Oh, snowy-breasted pearl,
May I never from the fair
        With life return.

20

Since the first part of our book refers mainly to translations from old Irish song-lyrics it may be excusable to give such a lyric and place it side by side with a good translation which would give readers the opportunity to compare them if they wish to do so. The one I have chosen is a modern translation by the poet Riobárd O Fearacháin, until recently Director of Radio Eireann, and the Irish song was by a vagabond named Seán O Coileán (1754-1817) who came from near Clonakilty in West Cork and is probably best known from schooldays as the author of *Tigh Molaga* an elegy in the style of Grey on the old Abbey at Timoleague. He was intended for the priesthood, for which he would obviously have been unsuitable, and when this proved abortive, became a hedge schoolmaster. His life was notorious; he had four children by his wife, and several others by her sister with whom he lived openly. Both eventually left him, and as a parting gesture the sister burned down his house and manuscripts. He died in poverty in Skibbereen, and was buried at Kilmeen, near the Timoleague Abbey of which he wrote.

7. MÁIRÍN DE BARRA

Words: Seán Ó Coileán
Air: Traditional—Origin unknown

A Mháirín de Barra, do mharaigh tú m'intinn,
do chuir tú beo i dtalamh mé i gan fhios dom 'mhuintir,
Ar mo luí dhom ar mo leaba is ort 'sea bhím ag cuimhneamh
is ar m'éirí dhom ar maidin mar gur chealg tú an croí dom.

Do thugas is thugas is thugas om' chroí greann duit
Ar Dhomhnach Fhéile Mhuire na gCoinneal sa teampall,
is do shúilín ba ghlaise ná uisce na ngeamhartha
is do bhéilín ba bhinne ná an druid nuair a labhrann.

Do shíl mé tú a mhealladh le briathra is le póga
do shíl mé tú a mhealladh le leabhair is le móide
Is do shíl mé tú a mhealladh ar bhreacadh na heornan
ach d'fhag tú dubhach dealbh ar theacht don bliain nua mé.

21

Is aoibhinn don talmah go siúlann tú féin air
Is aoibhinn don talamh an uair a sheineann tú véarsa
Is aoibhinn don leaba ina luíonn tú fé éadach,
is aoibhinn don bhfear a gheobhaidh tú mar chéile.

8. MÁIRÍN DE BARRA
(English Version)

Words: Riobárd Ó Faracháin
Air: Máirín de Barra

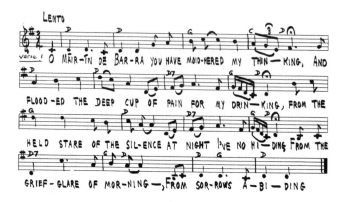

I gave and I gave and I gave without stinting
On Candlemas Day in the church my heart's minting
For your eyes' smiling, grayer than corn-ears dew pearlings
And your mouth's singing, gayer than the dawn talk of
[starlings.

With wile I'd have won you, with kiss and with wooing
With wile I'd have won you, with silence and suing.
With wile I'd have won you, when the barley was turning
But the blade was but sprung when you left me love
[mourning.

I envy the road that rings sweet to your treading
I envy the wind that your thyme-breath is wedding
I envy the pillow your sloe-head clouds over
And I envy to crazing of envy your lover.

22

I'd go and I'd go on through full lands and lonely
I'd rove over seas with no wealth but you only
If my clay the clay-quilt of the grave-bed lay under
And you said you were mine, I would rend   earth asunder.

O Máirín you've made me the jest at the reaping
The tale of the market, the show for the peeping
The corn for the flailing of tongues at the threshing
The hound that the switch of their laughter is lashing.

*You will note we have given a fuller version in English than
in the Irish text.*

9. THE BRINK OF THE WHITE ROCK

Words: Trans. by William Blacker (1777-1855)
from unknown Irish of c. 1650
Air: Ar Bruach na Carraige Báine

By yonder stream a maiden dwells, Who every other
maid excels; Less fair the swan in snowy pride, That
graceful stems sweet Banna's tide, The leech in vain would
seek to cure, The pangs of soul—that I endure since
of each joy and hope bereft, That stately fair— my
sight has left

Oh, were each earthly treasure mine,
For you I would it all resign;
Each fond regret my ardent love
Shall place my dear one far above.

23

Come, maiden, where, beyond the sea,
Both health and riches wait on thee;
Repress each lingering thought that stays
On home, and friends, and Carrick Braes.

Lov'd charmer of the flaxen hair,
I'll deck thee forth with anxious care;
All dressed in silken sheen so fine,
The costliest in the land to shine;
While rings of gold adorn thy hands,
And menials wait on thy commands;
And friends behold, on fond amaze,
Thy splendour upon Carrick Braes.

Joyce, Walsh and O'Daly gave different versions of the air. I have selected a simplified version of O'Daly as being the oldest, and, to me, the most tuneful. The air Davis used for *The West's Asleep* was taken from Bunting and named there *The Brink of the White Rock*. It, too, suits this song very well. The original is said to have been an Epitalamium or 'Welcome Home' song for Elizabeth Blacker, who married the Hon. Robert Stuart of Tyrone around 1666. The Blacker family were large landowners near Portadown in County Armagh.

10. HAVE YOU BEEN TO CARRICK?

Words: Edward Walsh from Irish of Dominic O'Mongan
Air: An Raibh tú ag an gCarraig?

HAVE YOU BEEN AT CAR-RICK, AND SAW YOU MY TRUE LOVE THERE —! AND SAW YOU HER FEA-TURES, ALL BEAU-TI — FUL BRIGHT —, AND FAIR ——! SAW YOU THE MOST FRAG ——RANT FLOW-RING SWEET AP——PLE TREE ——!

24

I have been at Carrick, and saw thy own true love there;
And saw, too, her features, all beautiful, bright, and fair;
And saw the most fragrant, flow'ring, sweet apple-tree —
I saw they lov'd one — she pines not in grief, like thee!

The air is that generally used for the Irish song nowadays.
The song was composed early in the eighteenth century for
another member of the Blacker family—Eliza—who later
became Lady Dunken of Bushmills. Dominic Mongan was a
gentleman bard of Co. Tyrone, blind from birth.

Now for one of the loveliest of Irish airs, the origin of
which is doubtful and for which there are several different,
fragmentary versions of the song. I have taken the liberty of
making a translation as nothing available seemed appropriate.
I can only hope it won't seem inadequate when compared
to the beauty of the tune.

11. THE COOLUN

Words: Translated from the old song by James N. Healy
Music: An Chúil Fhionn

Did you see my fair one
    a-walking on the roadway,
And she stepping with dainty footwear
    through the early dewy day?
And 'tho blue-eyed youths hunger
    as she passes them there
They could never be worthy to
    marry my fair.

Did you see my Coolun
    on a fine day alone,
Hair gleaming on her shoulder
    her cheek as rose unblown?
And the fragrance of honey
    will follow her way.
Let no man unfriendly
    offend her this day.

Did you see my beauty
    down by the waves there,
Gold rings on her fingers
    and she fixing her hair?
Power, who owns that fine ship
    by the quay,
Swore he'd wish to have my Coolun
    than have all Ireland free.

The original song has been attributed to a priest, Oliver
O'Hanley, a Gaelic poet of c. 1700-1750, and written in
praise of a County Limerick Beauty named Nellie O'Grady.
It would, however, be impossible to say which, if any, of
the varied Irish versions are his. The tune may have been
older than his time and then renamed after his song. Some
authorities attribute the air to Muiris Ua Duagain, an Irish
bard from Benburb in Co. Tyrone near the middle of the
seventeenth century; but the truth in respect of these
speculations is that, in the absence of documentary proof,
we do not know.

Some of the difficulties facing collectors of old Irish songs is the variety of tunes which have been used for some of them. It is a problem which is not uncommon, and which collectors must be prepared to deal with. So, for the old song which follows—a translation of *An Páistín Fionn (My Fair Haired Young Girl)*— and I may add that there are further available airs for this one song alone! It might not be unreasonable to leave the problem, for this once, to the reader and let him, or her, decide a personal preference. The following are the sources of the four airs printed:

1) A Waterford version of the air, as collected by an tAthair Pádraig Breathnach.

2) That used by Sir Samuel Ferguson when translating the song.

3) The version used by O'Daly in his *Poets and Poetry of Munster* for a translation by James Clarence Mangan. O'Daly's musical arrangements are usually rather florid. He also gives an interesting Tipperary version of the song.

4) Horncastle's version from his *Music of Ireland*, 1844. For this, in his *Minstrelsy of Ireland*, 1831, he used a translation by John D'Alton.

The translation I am giving is that of Sir Samuel Ferguson, which would seem to be the most appealing as a singable version today; however, it is fair to say that the translation by Edward Walsh is very similar, and almost equal in merit.

27

DEAR, AND MY FAIR — LOVE —; YOU ARE MY OWN DEAR AND MY FOND-EST HOPE
HERE —, AND O —; THAT MY COT-TAGE YOU SHARE — LOVE —.

12. PASTHEEN FIONN

Words: From the Irish, by Sir Samuel Ferguson
Air: An Páistín Fionn

OH MY FAIR PAS-THEEN IS MY HEARTS DE-LIGHT HER GAY HEART LAUGHS IN HER
BLUE EYE BRIGHT, LIKE THE AP-PLE BLOS-SOM HER BO-SOM WHITE, AND HER
NECK LIKE THE SWAN'S ON A MARCH MORN BRIGHT, THEN O-RO WILL YOU COME WITH ME
COME WITH ME, COME WITH ME? O-RO WILL YOU COME WITH ME BROWN GIRL SWEET? FOR
OH! I WOULD GO THRO' SNOW AND SLEET, IF YOU WOULD BUT COME WITH ME
BROWN GIRL SWEET —.

Love of my heart, my fair Pastheen!
Her cheeks are as red as the rose's sheen;
But my lips have tasted no more, I ween,
Than the glass I drank to the health of my queen!
Chorus.

Were I in the town, where's mirth and glee,
Or 'twixt two barrels of barley bree,
With my fair Pastheen upon my knee,
'Tis I would drink to her pleasantly!
Chorus.

28

Nine nights I lay in longing and pain,
Betwixt two bushes, beneath the rain,
Thinking to see you, love, once again;
But whistle and call were all in vain!
Chorus.

I'll leave my people, both friend and foe;
From all the girls in the world I'll go;
But from you, sweetheart, oh, never! oh no!
Till I lie in the coffin, stretched cold and low!
Chorus.

Douglas Hyde thinks that the version we have of the song is a much altered one of the original, which he things concerns some *cladhaire* or rogue, who came to carry off a girl, but took the wrong one. Hardiman's version is altogether different from that of Hyde, which, since two good researchers were involved, merely goes to show what has been said earlier — it is very difficult to be definitive about many of the old songs, which were transmitted orally and in increasingly varying versions from generation to generation in different parts of the country. There was the added difficulty when the time came to collect them that the language was dying in some of the areas involved, and the true meaning or story behind the song had been lost. O'Daly, perhaps erroneously, put the author down as Seámus Mhic Consaidín (James Considine) of Sheepford, Co. Clare (late eighteenth century). Another tradition suggests that the song referred to the son of James II in its original form.

Possibly the oldest love song which we have in approximately the form in which it was written is *Eileen Aroon*. It has an interesting history. Cearbhaill O Dálaigh was a harper of the early seventeenth century. The tradition goes that the lady of his heart was to be married to another, and that he disguised himself so that he would pass unnoticed amongst those gathering for the feast. He had composed this song and when he sang it she, recognising his voice, joined him and they eloped together.

The music later became well known to different words, when it was 'borrowed' for the song about Robin Adair.

13. EILEEN AROON

Words: Gerald Griffin
Air: Eibhlín a Rúin (Ó Dálaigh)

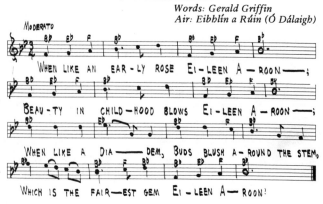

WHEN LIKE AN EAR-LY ROSE EI-LEEN A-ROON——;

BEAU-TY IN CHILD-HOOD BLOWS EI-LEEN A-ROON——;

WHEN LIKE A DIA——DEM, BUDS BLUSH A-ROUND THE STEM,

WHICH IS THE FAIR——EST GEM EI-LEEN A-ROON?

When I am far away,
    Eileen Aroon,
Be gayest of the gay,
    Eileen Aroon.
Too dear your happiness,
For me to wish it less —
Love has no selfishness,
    Eileen Aroon.

And it must be our pride
    Eileen Aroon.
Our trusting tears to hide,
    Eileen Aroon.
They wish our love to blight,
We'll wait for Fortune's light —
The flowers close up at night.
    Eileen Aroon.

And when we meet alone,
    Eileen Aroon,
Upon my bosom thrown
    Eileen Aroon.
That hour with light bedecked,
Shall cheer us and direct,
A beacon to the wrecked,
    Eileen Aroon.

Fortune, thus sought, will come,
    Eileen Aroon.
We'll win a happy home,
    Eileen Aroon.
And, as it slowly rose,
'Twill tranquilly repose,
A rock 'mid melting snows.
    Eileen Aroon.

Eileen Aroon (Eibhlín a Rúin): — Eileen, my love.

Although the meaning in English may not have been understood, Irish song was known and popular in England as far back as Shakespeare's day. One of his characters in Henry IV — the ebullient Pistol — refers in gibberish to a song later called *Calleno Custorame* which has been recognised as *Cailín ó chois Siúire mé (I'm a girl from the River Suir)*. During the eighteenth century Irish tunes were freely borrowed for the popular Ballad Operas, such as *The Beggars Opera*. One such love song was written by an Englishman, George Colman the Younger (1762-1836) for his musical drama entitled *The Surrender of Calais* to a tune which had already been known as *Savourneen Deelish*, but which has now been forgotten — probably because Colman's song was successful and obliterated the memory of any words which had gone before them.

14. SAVOURNEEN DEELISH

Words: George Colman, the Younger
Air: Savourneen Dílis

OH! THE MO-MENT WAS SAD WHEN MY LOVE AND I PART-ED SA-VOUR-NEEN DEE-LISH, EI-LEEN OGE! AS I KISSD OFF HER TEARS I WAS NIGH BRO-KEN HEAR-TED, SA-VOUR-NEEN DEE-LISH, EI-LEEN — OGE! WAN WAS HER CHEEK WHICH HUNG ON MY SHOUL-DER DAMP WAS HER HAND, NO MAR-BLE WAS COLD-ER I FELT THAT I NE-VER A-GAIN SHOULD BE-HOLD HER, SA-VOUR-NEEN DEE-LISH EI-LEEN — OGE!

As a noble ship I've seen
  Sailing o'er the swelling billow,
So I've marked the graceful mien
  Of lovely Kate of Garnavilla.
    Have you been, &c.

If poet's prayers can banish cares,
  No cares shall come to Garnavilla;
Joy's bright rays shall gild her days,
  And dove-like peace perch on her pillow.
    Charming maid of Garnavilla!
    Lovely maid of Garnavilla!
    Beauty, grace, and virtue wait
    Oh lovely Kate of Garnavilla.

'Kate' was Catherine Helen Nagle (1783-1862) of Garnavilla House, near Cahir in Tipperary. She afterwards married Richard Fitzgerald of Muckridge, who in his obituary of 1840 was described as a descendant of the Fifth Earl of Kildare. They had twelve children.

Lysaght was one of those who frequented the Spa in Mallow when it was a fashionable resort of 'The Rakes', and the song about those gentlemen is also attributed to him. The Nagles were related to the family of that name from Kilavullen, near Mallow.

So we come to Thomas Moore.

18. LOVE THEE DEAREST

Words: Thomas Moore

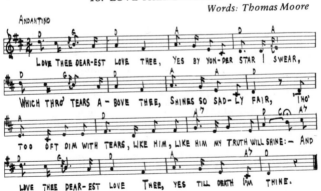

Leave thee, dearest? Leave thee?
　No, that star is not more true;
When my vows deceive thee
　He will wander, too.
A cloud of night may veil his light,
　And death shall darken mine,
But — leave thee, dearest? Leave thee?
　No, 'till death I'm thine!

　　Thomas Moore (1779-1852) was born in Aungier Street, Dublin, the son of a grocer. He was educated by Samuel Whyte who had taught Sheridan, and graduated from Trinity with a B.A. in 1799. He left Dublin to study law in London, but had been publishing poems since the age of thirteen. The first numbers of his *Irish Melodies* were published in 1807 and at intervals thereafter, bringing him fame both as their originator and performer, for he had a pleasant voice, and as a result had a particular social success. It was because of his image as a 'drawing-room entertainer' who was only concerned with monetary success that he was regarded with some scorn by the nationalistically minded writers of the years after his own—particularly when the events of the Fenian time had stirred men's minds. It was also considered, and there must be some truth admitted in this, that he bastardised the spirit of the original tunes and gave them a soppiness which ruined their character. However, it is also fair to say that he took much of the music, almost note for note, from Bunting and other collectors, and did not himself change as much as he has been accused of doing. Neither was he unpatriotic. It would be hard to find a line of his which decries his own country, and many of his 'melodies' such as *The Minstrel Boy* and *Let Erin Remember* are candid enough to have raised an enquiring eyebrow in the drawing-rooms where he found such favour. He was a fellow student and friend of Robert Emmet, and may have been close to being caught up in that young man's activities. One of his best love songs concerns the love of Sarah Curran for Emmet and her grief at his tragic fate.

19. SHE IS FAR FROM THE LAND

Words: Thomas Moore
Air: Original to Open the Door,
now more familiar to air by Frank Lambert (1897)

1. She is far from the land — where her young hero sleeps, And lovers around her are sigh — ing; But coldly she turns — from their gaze — and weeps — for her heart — in his grave is ly — ing —

2. (She) sings the wild songs — of her dear native plains, Ev'ry note which he loved — a — wak — ing. Ah little they think — who delight in her strains

She — how the heart — of the minstrel is break — ing — He liv'd for his love — for his country he died —; they were all that to life had en-twined — him —; Nor soon shall the tears — of his country be dried — Nor long — will his love stay be-hind — him — Nor — long — will his love stay be — hind — him —

Oh! make her a grave where the sunbeams rest,
  When they promise a glorious morrow;
They'll shine o'er her sleep like a smile from the West,
  From her own lov'd island of sorrow.

39

It has also been thought of Moore that his songs were only written for the occasion with little real meaning behind them. This to some extent might have been true when there was the necessity to provide new songs through sheer commercial necessity; but at least one song belies the truth of this being a blanket assertion.

In 1811 he married Bessie Dyke in London. Whatever looks she may have had were ruined by a skin disease after they had been married for some time, and she feared that as a result she might lose his affection. His reply was to write one of the most beautiful love songs of all time to her as reassurance. Perhaps it is one of those songs which you know so well as to take for granted; if so, read the lyric again, and consider the thought behind the reason for its being written.

20. BELIEVE ME IF ALL THOSE ENDEARING CHARMS

Words: Thomas Moore
Air: My Lodging is on the cold ground

It is not while beauty and youth are thine own,
And thy cheeks unprofaned by a tear,
That the fervour and faith of a soul can be known
To which time will but make thee more dear.
Oh! the heart that has truly loved never forgets,
But as truly loves on to the close, —
As the sunflower turns on her God when he sets,
The same look that she gave when he rose.

Many people have been harsh critics of Moore since his death, but one wonders how many of them could match the consistency of his writing. However, the atmosphere in the country before and during Young Irelander and Fenian days, and in particular the emergence of *The Nation* paper encouraged the writing of songs which had to do with love of country rather than of the fair sex. Here then are two of these writers. John Keegan Casey ('Leo') (1846-1870) wrote *The Rising of the Moon* in his teens and was later jailed for his nationalistic activities. His early death was attributed to the harsh treatment he received in prison, but Casey's verse, while strong, is seldom bitter, and he wrote with an easy, attractive style. He was released on condition that he left the country, but instead he disguised himself as a Quaker, called himself Hamilton, and continued to operate from a lodging in the shadow of Dublin Castle. But time had run out on him: he was dead in less than six months from leaving the jail. He wrote the song we quote, free from political consideration, for Mary Briscoe of Castlerea whom he married in 1867.

21. MAIRE MY GIRL

Words: John Keegan Casey
Original air: Maighréad Ní Cheallaigh
Later music by: George Aitken

O-VER THE DIM BLUE HILLS STRAYS A WILD RI-VER —; O-VER THE

DIM BLUE HILLS RESTS MY HEART E-VER — . DEAR-ER AND BRIGHT-ER THAN

41

JEW-ELS AND PEARL——, DWELLS SHE IN BEAU-TY THERE, MAi—RE MY GIRL——,

DWELLS SHE IN BEAU-TY THERE, MAi—RE MY GIRL——.

Down upon Claris heath shines the soft berry,
  On the brown harvest tree droops the red cherry.
Sweeter the honey lips, softer the curl,
  Straying adown thy cheeks, Maire my girl.

'Twas on an April eve that I first met her;
  Many an eve shall pass ere I forget her.
Since my young heart has been wrapped in a whirl,
  Thinking and dreaming of Maire my girl.

She is too kind and fond ever to grieve me,
  She has too pure a heart e'er to deceive me.
Were I Tyrconnell's chief or Desmond's earl,
  Life would be dark, wanting Maire my girl.

Over the dim blue hills strays a wild river,
  Over the dim blue hills rest my heart ever.
Fairer and dearer than jewel or pearl,
  Dwells she in beauty there, Maire my girl.

Casey's song was used for an early 'talkie', and the new air
written for it at that time brought it renewed popularity.

Although he later became a successful businessman, and
one of the founders of the Cork Historical and Archaeolo-
gical Society late in a long life, Denny Lane (1818-1895)
was also in trouble over his political views early in life. He
was a Young Irelander and wrote for *The Nation*: his two
best remembered songs, both charming, appeared in it.
They were *Kate of Araglen* (1844) and the beautiful *Carrigdhoun* in the following year. The songs were written over
the name 'Domhnall na Gleanna'.

22. KATE OF ARAGLEN

Words: Denny Lane
*Air: original, a version of 'An Cailín Rua'; this version
arranged by James N. Healy from 'Rodney's Glory'*

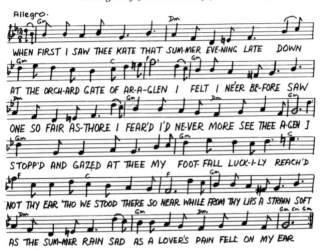

WHEN FIRST I SAW THEE KATE THAT SUM-MER EVE-NING LATE DOWN
AT THE ORCH-ARD GATE OF AR-A-GLEN I FELT I NE'ER BE-FORE SAW
ONE SO FAIR AS-THORE I FEAR'D I'D NE-VER MORE SEE THEE A-GEN I
STOPP'D AND GAZED AT THEE MY FOOT-FALL LUCK-I-LY REACH'D
NOT THY EAR 'THO WE STOOD THERE SO NEAR WHILE FROM THY LIPS A STRAIN SOFT
AS THE SUM-MER RAIN SAD AS A LOVER'S PAIN FELL ON MY EAR

I've heard the lark in June
The harp's wild plaintive tune,
The thrush, that aye too soon
   Gives o'er his strain;
I've heard, in hush'd delight
The mellow horn at night
Waking the echoes light
   Of wild Loch Lein;
But neither echoing horn,
Nor thrush upon the thorn,
Nor lark at early morn
   Hymning in air,
Nor harper's lay divine,
E'er witch'd this heart of mine
Like that sweet voice of thine,
   That evening there.

43

And now you're mine alone,
That heart is all my own —
That heart, that ne'er hath known
    A flame before,
That form, of mould divine,
That snowy hand of thine,
Those locks of gold are mine
    For evermore.
Was lover ever seen
As blest as thine, Caithlin?
Hath ever lover been
    More fond, more true?
Thine is my ev'ry vow!
For ever dear, as now!
Queen of my heart be thou!
    My Colleen Rua.

Denny Lane wrote *Kate of Araglen* to the air of *An Cailín Rua* but I found it rather difficult to fit it to any of the available airs of that name, so, with some adjustments to the melody, found that it goes fairly well to *Rodney's Glory*.

23. CARRIGDHOUN
(*Lament of the Irish Maiden*)

Words: Denny Lane
Music: Traditional

THE HEATH WAS GREEN IN CARR-IG-DHOUN —, BRIGHT SHONE THE SUN ON ARD-NA-LEE —; THE DARK GREEN TREES BENT TREM-BLING DOWN —, TO KISS THE SLUM-BER-ING OWN-A-BEE ———, THAT HAPPY DAY —, 'TWAS BUT LAST MAY —, 'TIS LIKE A DREAM TO ME ———, WHEN DOMH-NAL SWORE AYE, OE'R AND OE'R ———, WE'LL PART NO MORE A- -STÓR MO CHROIDHE !

44

On Carrigdhoun the heath is brown,
    The clouds are dark over Ardnalee,
And many a stream comes rushing down
    To swell the angry Owenabwee.
The moaning blast is sweeping fast
    Thru' many a leafless tree,
And I'm alone, for he is gone,
    My hawk is flown, ochone machree!

Soft April showers and bright May flowers
    Will bring the summer back again;
But will they bring me back the hours
    I spent with my brave Domhal then?
'Tis but a chance, for he's gone to France
    To wear the fleur-de-lis;
But I'll follow you, my Domhnal dhu,
    For still I'm true to you, a chroidhe

Ochone machree (ochón, mo chroidhe):- alas, my heart
Domhnal dhu: – my black Donal
A chroidhe: – my heart.

The air of *Carrigdhoun* was used, with changes of rhythm
and form, by Houston Collisson later for Percy French's
Mountains of Mourne. Lane may have intended the song to
be sung to *The Blackbird*, but it is now generally loved to
the above air.

24. SHE LIVED BESIDE THE ANNER
Words: Charles J. Kickham

SHE LIVED BE-SIDE THE AN-NER AT THE FOOT OF SlIEVE-NA- MON A

GEN-TLE I-RISH COL-LEEN WITH MILD EYES LIKE THE DAWN HER

LIPS WERE DE-WY ROSE-BUDS HER — TEETH WERE PE-ARLS RARE AND A

SNOW-DRIFT 'NEATH A BEECH-EN BOUGH HER NECK AND NUT-BROWN HAIR

45

How pleasant 'twas to see her
    On a Sunday when the bell
Was filling with its mellow tones
    Lone wood and grassy dell!
And when at eve young maidens
    Strayed the river banks along,
The widow's brown-haired daughter
    Was the loveliest of the throng.

O brave, brave Irish girls!
    We well may call you brave —
Sure the least of all your perils
    Is the stormy ocean wave
When you leave your quiet valleys,
    And cross th' Atlantic foam,
To hoard your hard-won earnings
    For the helpless one at home.

'Write word to my own dear mother,
    Say we'll meet with God above;
And tell my little brothers
    I send them all my love;
May angels ever guard them'
    Is their dying sister's prayer —
And folded in the letter
    Was a braid of nut-brown hair.

Ah, cold and well-nigh callous
    This weary heart has grown,
For thy helpless fate, dear Ireland,
    And for sorrows of my own;
Yet a tear my eye will moisten
    When by the Anner side I stray,
For the lily of the mountain foot
    That withered far away.

Charles J. Kickham (b. Mullinahone, Co. Tipperary 1828 —
d. Blackrock, Co. Dublin 1882) was another Nationalistic
writer who suffered for his political views. His eyesight was
seriously affected while in prison. His best song is probably
Slievenamon.

25. THE MAID OF SLIEVENAMON

Words: Charles J. Kickham
Music: Sliabh na mban Fionn

It was not the grace of her queenly air,
   Nor her cheek of the rose's glow,
Nor her soft black eyes, nor her flowing hair,
   Nor was it her lily-white brow.
'Twas the soul of truth, and of melting ruth,
   And the smile like a summer dawn,
That stole my heart away, one mild summer day,
   In the valley near Slievenamon.

In the festive hall, by the star-watch'd shore,
   My restless spirit cries:
'My love, oh my love, shall I ne'er see you more,
   And, my land, will you ever uprise?'
By night and by day I ever, ever pray,
   While lonely my life flows on,
To see our flag unrolled, and my true love to enfold,
   In the valley near Slievenamon.

I first heard Slievenamon as a teenager from a farm
labourer who was plastered after a day at the harvest. He
grasped my hand and wouldn't let it go until he had sub-
jected me to every verse, delivered with great emphasis and

47

stressing almost every word with a handshake. It was in an unlikely place, 'Hodders' at Fountainstown, where more genteel accents were normally to be heard. Nevertheless the cadence of the song remained in my mind.

By the middle of the last century considerable research work had been added to the pioneering of Bunting in salvaging Irish tunes which might otherwise have been forgotten. Petrie, already mentioned, did invaluable work, as did Forde, Pigot and many more.

Patrick W. Joyce (1827-1914) made two important collections in which he included many songs from the countryside—particularly in the area of North Munster—which might otherwise have been forgotten. One of them was a very pleasant love comment, with a touch of consoling cynicism.

26. FAIR MAIDEN'S BEAUTY

Words: Collected by P. W. Joyce
Air: Traditional

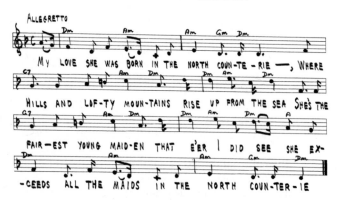

My love is as bright as a morning in May,
My love is as pure as the sweet new-mown hay;
I love her in my bosom's core and she fancies me;
We're the happiest pair in the north counterie.

My love is as sweet as the cinnamon tree;
She clings to me as close as the bark to the tree;
But the leaves they will wither and the roots will decay,
And fair maiden's beauty will soon fade away.

Joyce got the above song from his father who heard it about 1840 being sung at the other side of the river by Tom Long, 'a splendid singer with a baritone voice.' The other reapers put down their implements to listen, and when the song was over they resumed their work.

Samuel Ferguson (1810-1878), who was knighted in 1875, was a good poet whose work closely followed the music researchers in translating song. He expressed many of the old legends in verse. We remember him here, however, by a simple and very beautiful original lyric to an old tune. My friend the late Frank Ryan used to sing it with fine feeling.

27. THE LARK IN THE CLEAR AIR

Words: Sir Samuel Ferguson
Air: An Táilliúir (The Tailor)

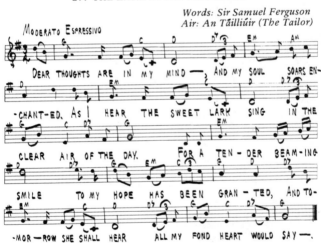

I shall tell her all my love, all my soul's adoration,
And I think she will hear me, and will not say me nay.
It is this that gives my soul all its joyous elation,
As I hear the sweet lark sing in the clear air of the day.

The legal profession had several members with a pretty turn for verse early in that century. John F. Waller (b. Limerick 1809 of Tipperary family — d. England 1894) should not be forgotten because of two songs: *Kitty Neal*, which is in my *Second Book of Ballads*, and above all the beautifully rhythmic *Spinning Wheel*. Advice to singer: keep the tempo moving to that of a spinning wheel, and don't slow down until the wheel itself slows in the last verse. Delia Murphy in the '40's made the song popular from her recording; she may have had a rough voice but there was marvellous rhythm in it.

28. THE SPINNING WHEEL

Words: John F. Waller

'What's that noise that I hear at the window, I wonder?'
''Tis the little birds chirping the holly-bush under.'
'What makes you be shoving and moving your stool on,
And singing, all wrong, that old song of "The Coolun"?'

There's a form at the casement—the form of her true love—
And he whispers, with face bent: 'I'm waiting for you, love:
Get up from the stool, through the lattice step lightly,
We'll rove in the grove while the moon's shining brightly.'

Merrily, cheerily, noiselessly whirring,
Spins the wheel, rings the reel, while the foot's stirring:
Sprightly, and lightly, and airily ringing,
Trills the sweet voice of the young maiden singing.

The maid shakes her head, on her lip lays her fingers,
Steals up from the stool—longs to go, and yet lingers;
A frightened glance turns to her drowsy grandmother,
Puts one foot on the stool, spins the wheel with the other.

Lazily, easily, swings now the wheel round.
Slowly and lowly is heard now the reel's sound;
Noiseless and light to the lattice above her,
The maid steps—then leaps to the arms of her lover.

Slower—and slower—and slower the wheel swings;
Lower—and lower—and lower the reel rings;
Ere the reel and the wheel stop their ringing and moving,
Through the grove the young lovers by moonlight are roving.

Another scholar who dabbled in Irish song-writing to the effect of leaving us, among heavier writing, a simple Irish love song, was John Todhunter of Quaker parentage (b. Dublin 1839 – d. 1916), a doctor of medicine who gave up that career for literature. Through the Gaelic League in London he was one of those interested in the promotion of the Irish language.

29. AGHADOE

Words & Air: John Todhunter

There's a glade in A-gha-doe —, A-gha-doe A-gha-doe — There's a
sweet and si-lent glade in A-gha-doe where we met my love and
I —, Love's bright pla-net in the sky, In that sweet and si-lent
glade in A-gha-doe. There's a glen in A-gha-doe —, A-gha-
doe A-gha-doe —, There's a deep and se-cret glen in A-gha-
doe where I hid him from the eyes — of the red coats and their
spies —, That year the trou-ble came to A-gha-doe —.

But they tracked me to that glen in Aghadoe, Aghadoe,
    When the price was on his head in Aghadoe,
O'er the mountains, through the wood, as I stole to him with
    And their bullets found his heart in Aghadoe.   [food,
I walked to Mallow Town from Aghadoe, Aghadoe,
    Brought his head from the gaol's gate to Aghadoe,
Then I covered him with fern and I piled on him the cairn;
    Like an Irish king he sleeps in Aghadoe.

    Side by side with scholarly research, translations and
original writing, another tradition of song writing about the
fair sex had developed from among the anonymous writers
of the street corners and the fields. These were, perhaps,
the true successors of those who had given us our rich heri-
tage of Irish language songs.

52

30. THE MAID OF SWEET GURTEEN

Words & Air: Traditional

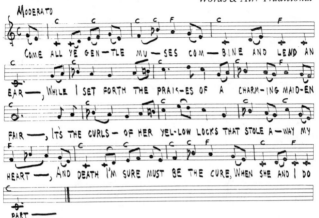

COME ALL YE GEN-TLE MU-SES COM-BINE AND LEND AN
EAR —, WHILE I SET FORTH THE PRAIS-ES OF A CHARM-ING MAID-EN
FAIR —, IT'S THE CURLS — OF HER YEL-LOW LOCKS THAT STOLE A-WAY MY
HEART —, AND DEATH I'M SURE MUST BE THE CURE, WHEN SHE AND I DO
PART —

The praises of this lovely maid I mean for to unfold,
Her hair hangs o'er her shoulders like lovely links of gold.
Her carriage neat, her limbs complete, which fractured quite
my brain,
Her skin is whiter than the swan that swims on the purling
stream.

Her eyes are like the diamonds that shine with crystal sheen
So modest and so tender she's fit to be a queen,
How many pleasant hours I spent all in the garden field,
She's won my heart, I cannot part with the maid of sweet
Gurteen.

It was my cruel father that caused my grief and woe.
For he took and locked her in a room and would not let her
go.
Her windows I have daily watched, thinking she might be seen
In hopes some time to get a sight of the maid of sweet
Gurteen.

My father he arose one day and this to me did say
Oh son, dear son, be advised by me, don't throw yourself
away

For to marry a poor servant girl whose parents are so mean,
So stay at home and do not roam, but always with me
remain.

O father, dearest father, don't deprive me of my dear,
I would not lose my darling for a thousand pounds a year.
Was I possessed of England's crown I would make her my
queen,
In high renown I'd wear the crown with the maid of sweet
Gurteen.

My father in a passion flew, and this to me did say,
Since it is the cause within this place no longer she shall stay,
Mark what I say, from this very day you ne'er shall see her
face,
For I will send her far away unto some other place.

'Twas in a few days after that a horse he did prepare
And sent my darling far away to place I know not where,
I may go view my darling's room where oft times she has
been
In hopes to get another sight of the maid of sweet Gurteen.

Now to conclude and make an end, I take my pen in hand,
Young Johnny Reilly is my name, and Flower Hills my land,
The days I spent in merriment since my darling first I seen,
And while I live I'll always think of the maid of sweet
Gurteen.

Perhaps fifteen years from the day I wrote this book an
elderly man from up the country asked me could I find the
words of *Sweet Gurteen* for him, which he remembered
hearing when a boy nearly eighty years before. It took me
some time, but I found it, and heard afterwards that it gave
him some pleasure. Obviously somebody did originally
write these old songs and put them to airs, but in the
memories of their being sung around winter fires the origins
have been forgotten. They tell of many more different
aspects of love than the more formal compositions of the
scholars.

31. THE LAMENT OF HUGH REYNOLDS

Words: Author unknown
Air: Doire Briain

My name it is Hugh Reynolds I came of honest parents, Near Cavan I was born — as you may plainly see —, For the loving of a maid —, One Catherine McCabe —, My life has been betrayed, She's the dear maid to me —, The country was bewailing, My doleful situation, But still I'd expectation this maid would set me free —, But O, She was ungrateful Her parents prov'd deceitful An' tho' I lov'd her faithful, She's the dear maid to me —.

Young men and tender maidens, throughout this Irish nation,
Who hear my lamentation, I hope you'll pray for me;
The truth I will unfold, that my precious blood she sold,
In the grave I must lie cold; she's the dear maid to me.

For now my glass is run, my last hour it is come,
And I must die for love and the height of loyalty!
I thought it was no harm to embrace her in my arms,
Or take her from her parents; but she's the dear maid to me.

Adieu, my loving father, and you, my tender mother,
Farewell, my dearest brother, who has suffered sore for me
With irons I'm surrounded, in grief I lie confounded,
By perjury unbounded; she's the dear maid to me.

Now, I can say no more; to the Law-board I must go,
There to take my last farewell of my friends and counterie;
Many the angels, shining bright, receive my soul this night,
And convey me into heaven with the blessed Trinity.

This is one of a number of elopement ballads. Hugh Reynolds was executed in 1826 for housebreaking and the
attempted abduction of Catherine McCabe. The girl's uncle
was generally credited as being the vindictive inventor of
the plot whereby Reynolds was captured and convicted.
The girl herself was an apparently unwilling witness at the
trial. The gossips reported that 'Divine Vengeance' followed
the McCabes. The very severe sentence of execution for
such an offence seems barbarous today and public sympathy
at the time was more frequently than otherwise with the
abductor—often it was the case of a young Catholic farmer
becoming enamoured with a girl of a family with strong
Orange connections—this also applied in the *Ballad of Willy
Reilly* and *Charming Mary Neill*; also *John McGoldrick and
the Quaker's Daughter*. As in most execution ballads the
verses are supposed, for effect, to be written in the first
person. 'She's the dear girl to me' means 'She has cost me
dearly'; and it certainly was a fated sort of love!

The following song, also of a sorrowful love—although
with less practical cause—with a plaintive refrain, is in this
section because this writer, at least, cannot be sure who the
author was. A gentlewoman is suggested who (as in the case
of Purty Molly Bralligan) hesitated to put her name to it.
The rhyming of 'conceal' and 'O'Neale' would certainly
suggest that it came from the drawing-room.

32. TEDDY O'NEALE

I've come to the cabin he danc'd his wild jigs in, as neat a mud palace as ever was seen and considering it served to keep poultry and pigs in, I'm sure it was always most elegant clean! But now all about it seems lonely and dreary, all sad and all silent no piper no reel! Not even the sun thro' the casement is cheery, since I miss the dear darling boy, Teddy O'Neale.

I dreamt but last night, (Oh! bad luck to my dreaming,
I'd die if I thought 'twould come surely to pass.)
But I dreamt, while the tears, down my pillow were streaming,
That Teddy was courtin' another fair lass.
Och! did not I wake with a weeping and wailing,
The grief of that thought was too deep to conceal;
My mother cried 'Norah, child, what is your ailing?'
And all I could utter, was 'Teddy O'Neale'.

Shall I ever forget, when the big ship was ready
The moment had come, when my love must depart,
How I sobb'd like a spalpeen, 'Goodbye to you Teddy,'
With drops on my cheek and a stone at my heart.
He says 'tis to better his fortune he's roving,
But what would be gold, to the joy I would feel
If I saw him come back to me, honest and loving
Still poor, but my own darling Teddy O'Neale.

The bitterness of loving, or the art of wooing, inspires
lyric writers on the subject far more often, of course, than

57

the contentment or fulfillment of married life; those who have lost sing more plaintively than those who have won the battle.

The following little song has long been a favourite of my own. There are several variations, both in England and in Ireland; the following is the version which I have sung.

33. LOVE IS 'ASIN'

Words: This version by James N. Healy
Air: Traditional, arr. Healy

For love is asin', and love is plasin'
And love is a pleasure when first it's new
But love grows colder when it gets older
And it fades and dies like the mornin' dew.

I left my father, I left my mother;
I left my brothers, and my sisters too,
I left my friends and my kind relations
I left them all just to be with you.

But love and porter make a young man older
And love and whiskey make him old and grey
What can't be cured, love, must be endured, love;
And so I am bound for Amerikay.

But love is asin', and love is tasin'
And love is a pleasure when first its new
But love grows colder when it gets older
And it fades and dies like the mornin' dew.

A somewhat similar style of number with the same sad wistfulness is *Carrigfergus*. It is a peculiar remnant—obviously the surviving part of a longer song, and as as result the

58

words are not entirely clear in meaning. I have three versions, all different; and none of them tell the story completely; nevertheless the effect of sadness comes over very well—from the air and a certain interesting obscurity in the words. Carrigfergus is an old town on the northern side of Belfast Lough.

34. CARRIGFERGUS

Words: This version, James N. Healy
Air: Traditional, arr. Healy

I WISH I WAS IN CARR-IG-FER-GUS ON-LY FOR NIGHTS IN BAL-LY-GRANT. I WOULD SWIM O-VER THE DEEP-EST O-CEAN—, AND WITH MY LOVE THERE WOULD I STAND; BUT THE SEA IS WIDE AND I CAN'T SWIM O-VER, NOR DO I HAVE—THE WINGS TO FLY IF I COULD FIND ME A STAL-WART BOAT MAN TO FER-RY ME OV-ER TO MY LOVE TO DIE——.

Now in Kilkenny it is reported
They've marble stones there as black as ink
With Gold and Silver I would transport her,
But I'll sing no more now 'till I get a drink.
I'm drunk today, but then I'm seldom sober—
A handsome rover from town to town,
Ah! but I'm sick now my days are over,
Come all ye young lads and lay me down.

Emigration is hinted, at least, in *Love is 'Asin'*. It is clearly stated in a sweet song from the Eastern midlands. Bunclody lies under the shadow of Mount Leinster, in County Wexford, where the Clody river joins the Slaney.

35. THE STREAMS OF BUNCLODY

Words & Air: Traditional—Co. Wexford

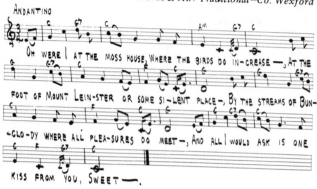

Oh, the streams of Bunclody they flow down so free
By the streams of Bunclody I'm longing to be,
A drinking strong liquor in the height of my cheer,
Here's health to Bunclody and the lass I love dear.

The cuckoo is a pretty bird, it sings as it flies,
It brings us good tidings, and tells us no lies,
It sucks the young birds' eggs to make its voice clear
And the more it cries cuckoo the summer draws near.

If I was a clerk and could write a good hand,
I would write to my true-love that she might understand,
For I am a young fellow who is wounded in love
Once I lived in Bunclody, but now must remove.

If I was a lark and had wings I could fly
I would go to yon arbour where my love she does lie,
I'd proceed to yon arbour where my true love does lie,
And on her fond bosom contented I would die.

'Tis why my love slights me, as you may understand,
That she has a freehold and I have no land,
She has great store of riches, and a large sum of gold,
And everything fitting a house to uphold.

So fare you well father and my mother, adieu
My sister and brother farewell unto you,
I am bound for America my fortune to try,
When I think on Bunclody I'm ready to die.

The air of *Bunclody* is also used for the ballad of *Willie Leonard*.

The girls too had their troubles, and the wandering young men of their hearts to think about. This number also gained great popularity in the '40's from the singing of Delia Murphy.

36. IF I WAS A BLACKBIRD

Words & Air: Traditional Street Song

If I was a blackbird I'd whistle and sing
And I'd follow the ship that my true love sails in —, and
on the top rigging I'd there build my nest —, and I'd
pillow my head on his lily white breast.

He promised to take me to Donnybrook fair
To buy me red ribbons to bind up my hair.
And when he'd return from the ocean so wide
He'd take me and make me his own loving bride.
Chorus.

His parents they slight me and will not agree
That I and my sailor boy married should be.
But when he comes home I will greet him with joy
And I'll take to my bosom my dear sailor boy.
Chorus.

37. I ONCE LOVED A BOY

Words & Air: Traditional Street Song (Dublin area)

I once lov'd a boy, and a bonny, bonny boy,
And a boy that I thought was my own
But he loves another girl better than me,
And has taken his flight and is gone, and is gone,
And has taken his flight and is gone.

The girl that has taken my own bonny boy
Let her make of him all that she can
For whether he loves me, or loves me not,
I'll walk with my love now and then, now and then
I'll walk with my love now and then.

The words of the above were published in broadsheet form by Bartie Corcoran, the ballad-monger of Dublin, where it seems to have been at one time popular. Petrie published the air, which was noted from the singing of a servant girl of Smollett Holden, whose collection of Irish Airs dates from 1806.

The following is one of the most plaintive of the Anglo-Irish Ballads. It must be sung quietly and sincerely.

Words & Air: Traditional

The trees are grow-ing tall my love, the grass is grow-ing green -, and ma-ny's the cruel and bit-ter day, that I a-lone have seen -, It is a cruel and bit-ter night that I must lie a-lone -, Oh, the bon-ny boy was young, but was grow-ing - .

'Oh Father, my father, indeed
You did me wrong
For to go and get me married
To one who is so young,
He being only sixteen years
And I being twenty-one;
He's a bonny boy, but young —
And still growing.'

'My daughter, my daughter
I did not do you wrong
For to go and get you married
To one who is so young
He will be a match for you
When I am dead and gone
He's a bonny boy, he's young —
but he's growing.'

'Oh Father, my father,
I'll tell you what I'll do
I'll send my love to college
For another year or two
And all around his college cap
I'll tie a ribbon blue
Just to let the ladies know
That he's married.'

At evening when strolling
Down by the college wall
You'd see the young collegiates
A playing at the ball
You'd see him in amongst them there
The fairest of them all
He's my bonny boy, he's young,
But he's growing.

At the early age of sixteen years
He was a married man,
At seventeen the father of
A darling baby son
At eighteen years — t'was over —
O'er his grave the grass grew strong,
Cruel death put an end
To his growing.

I will buy my love a shroud
Of the ornamental brown
And whilst they are making it
My tears they will run down
That once I had a true love
But now he's dead and gone
And I'll mind his bonny boy —
While he's growing.

There was another side to love also — the girl who carried
her coquetry too far — to the extent that the victim was in
the end content to 'leave her where he found her' which
was at the foot of the Sweet Brown Knowe, or hillock. It is
a fairly universal ballad, but may have originated in the
northern part of the country.

39. THE SWEET BROWN KNOWE

Words & Air: Traditional

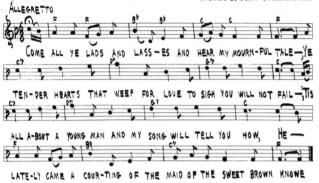

Come all ye lads and lass—es and hear my mourn—ful tale—ye
ten—der hearts that weep for love to sigh you will not fail—'tis
all a—bout a young man and my song will tell you how, he—
late—ly came a cour—ting of the maid of the sweet brown knowe

Said he, 'My pretty fair maid, will you come along with me,
We'll both go off together, and married we will be;
We'll join our hands in wedlock bands, I'm speaking to you
                                                                now,
And I'll do my best endeavour for the Maid of the Sweet
                                                    Brown Knowe.'

This fair and fickle young thing she knew not what to say;
Her eyes did shine like silver bright and merrily did play.
She said, 'Young man, your love subdue, for I am not ready
                                                                now,
And I'll spend another season at the foot of the Sweet
                                                    Brown Knowe.'

Said he, 'My pretty fair maid, how can you say so,
Look down on yonder valley, where my crops do gently grow;
Look down on yonder valley, where my horses and my plough
Are at their daily labour for the Maid of the Sweet Brown
                                                    Knowe.'

'If they're at their daily labour, kind sir, it's not for me;
For I've heard of your behaviour, I have indeed,' said she.
'There is an inn where you call in, I have heard the people
                                                                say,

Where you rap and call and pay for all, and go home at the
break of day.'

'If I rap and call and pay for all, the money is all my own;
And I'll never spend your fortune, for I hear that you have
got none
You thought you had my poor heart broke, in talking with
me now,'
So I left her where I found her at the foot of the Sweet
Brown Knowe.

If humour has its place in the love song bracket, what
more humorous than the lovers who want to express themselves to one another but cannot? Humorous to others,
perhaps, though hardly to themselves!

40. THE STUTTERING LOVERS

Words & Air: Traditional

Then out came the bonny wee lass
And she was O! so fair
And she went into the poor man's corn
To see if the birds were th-th-th-th-th-there, my lads,
To see if the birds were there.

And out came the brave young lad
And he was a fisherman's son,
And he went into the poor man's corn
To see where the lass had g-g-g-g-g-gone, my lads,
To see where the lass had gone.

He put his arm around her waist
He kissed her cheek and chin
Then out spake the bonny wee lass
'I fear it is a s-s-s-s-s-sin, my lad,
I fear it is a sin.'

He kissed her once and he kissed her twice
And he kissed her ten times o'er
'Twas fine to be kissing that bonny wee lass
That never was kissed bef-f-f-f-f-fore, my lads,
That never was kissed before.

The out came the poor old man
And he was tattered and torn
'Faith if that's the way ye're minding the corn
I'll mind it myself in the m-m-m-m-m-morn,' he said,
'I'll mind it myself in the morn.'

The air of the above may be of Scottish origin. It has
been used for several other songs. The song probably dates
from the beginning of the present century.

To end this section of unknown authors here is a ballad
of which there have been different versions. 'The Slaney'
has sometimes been used as a substitute river, but 'The Tanyard' is more generally accepted.

41. DOWN BY THE TANYARD SIDE

Words & Air: Traditional

I am a ram-blin' hay — ro, and by love I - am be-trayed, Near to the town of Bal - tin-glass, there dwells a love-ly maid, She's fair-er than Hy-path - ia bright and she's free from earth-ly pride, She's a dar - lin' maid her dwell-in' place is down by the Tan-yard side.

Her lovely hair in ringlets rare lies on her snow-white neck,
And the tender glances of her eyes would save a ship from
wreck.
Her two red lips so smiling and her teeth so pearly white,
Would make a man become her slave down by the Tanyard
side.

I courteously saluted her and I viewed her o'er and o'er,
And I said: 'Are you Aurora bright descending here below?'
'Oh, no, kind sir, I'm a maiden poor,' she modestly replied,
'And I daily labour for my bread down by the Tanyard side.'

So for twelve long years I courted her till at length we did
agree
For to acquaint her parents and married we would be.
But 'twas then her cruel father to me proved most unkind
Which makes me sail across the sea and leave my love behind.

Farewell, my aged parents, to you I bid adieu.
I'm crossing the main ocean all for the sake of you.
But whenever I return I will make her my bride,
And I'll roll her in my arms again down by the Tanyard side.

The performers of songs are almost as important as those
who write them; in that without performance a song is but

68

a still-born babe. If the writer is also the interpreter it adds
a special flavour. Moore was as well-known a performer of
his own *Melodies* as Carolan, with his harp, was of his.
Samuel Lover (1797-1868) wrote hundreds of songs, and
was one of the early 'one-man show' performers. His most
famous song was *The Low Back'd Car* (which is in my
Ballads from the Pubs of Ireland) but the one we are going
to give you is not now so well known, although it was once
a favourite. I have an old single-sided H.M.V. gramophone
record of the young John McCormack singing it, on which
the beautiful voice seems to come through a mist.

42. MOLLY BAWN

Words & Air: Samuel Lover

Now the pretty flowers were made to bloom, dear,
    And the pretty stars were made to shine,
And the pretty girls were made for boys' arms,
    And maybe you were made for mine.

The wicked watch-dog here is snarling,
    He takes me for a thief, you see,
For he knows, I'd steal you, Molly darling,
    And then transported I should be.

Oh, Molly Bawn, why leave me pining,
    All lonely, waiting here for you.
While the stars above are brightly shining.
    Because they have nothing else to do.
        Molly Bawn — Oh! Molly Bawn.

Late in the century came one of the greatest one-man show performers of all, singing his own songs to banjo accompaniment, telling stories and reciting poems; sketching and making pictures to the smoke of a candle. I have told his story in another book *Percy French and his Songs* but I will tell you here that he was Percy French (1854-1920) and his songs are as popular today as ever they were. Percy's lovers were generally careless and gay fellows and their philosophy was 'if you want 'em to run after you just look the other way', which is probably only too true. Here, however, we will let him tell the story of the wistful young man who sought *Little Brigid Flynn*.

43. LITTLE BRIGID FLYNN

Words & Air: Percy French

I've a nice slated house and a cow or two at grass, I've a plant garden running by the door —, I've a shelter for the hens and a stable for the ass, and what does a man want more —. I dunno —, maybe so —, and a bachelor is aisy and he's free —, but I've lots to look after and I'm living all alone and there's no one looking after me —.

Me father often tells me I should go and have a try
To get a girl that owns a bit of land;
I know the way he says it that there's someone in his eye,
And me mother has the whole thing planned.
I dunno, may be so,
And 'twould molify them greatly to agree,
But there's little Brigid Flynn,
Sure it's her I want to win,
Though she never throws an eye at me.

Oh! there's a little girl who is worth her weight in gold,
An' that's a dacent dowry don't you see;
And I mean to go and ax her as soon as I get bold,
If she'll come and have an eye to me.
I dunno — will she go,
But I'd like to have her sittin' on me knee,
And I'd sing like a thrush,
On a hawthorn bush
If she'll come and have an eye to me.

71

French came from the minor gentry, and was a surprising entry into the rough and tumble of show business. Johnny Patterson was born to it, and was at home in the Dublin 'Free-and-Easies'. He was born in Feakle in Co. Clare in 1840. He became well known as a circus clown and wrote songs such as *The Stone outside Dan Murphy's Door* and *Brigit Donoghue*, but his best-known song was the one which follows. He was killed in Tralee in 1889 when struck by an iron bar after a performance during which he sang a pro-Parnellite song.

44. THE GARDEN WHERE THE PRATIES GROW

Words & Music: Johnny Patterson

HAVE YOU EV-ER BEEN IN LOVE MY BOYS OR HAVE YOU FELT THE PAIN; I'D
SOON-ER BE IN JAIL MY-SELF THAN BE IN LOVE A-GAIN, FOR THE
GIRL I LOVE WAS BEAU-TI-FUL I'D HAVE YOU ALL TO KNOW AND I
MET HER IN THE GAR-DEN WHERE THE PRA-TIES GROW.

Chorus each time (music as verse):

She was just the sort of creature boys, that nature did intend
To walk right thru' the world, me boys, without the Grecian
Bend;
Nor did she wear a Chignon, I'd have you all to know —
And I met her in the garden where the praties grow.

Says I 'My pretty Kathleen I'm tired of single life,
And if you've no objection, sure I'll make you my sweet wife.'
She answered me quite modestly and curtsied very low,
'Oh you're welcome to the garden where the praties grow.'
Chorus.

72

Says I 'My pretty Kathleen, I hope that you'll agree,'
She was not like your city girls who say 'you're making free,'
Says she, 'I'll ax my parents, and tomorrow I'll let you know;
If you'll meet me in the garden where the praties grow.'
Chorus.

Oh the parents they consented and we're blessed with
                              children three,
Two boys just like their mother and girl the image of me,
And now we're going to train them up the way they ought
                              to go,
For to dig out in the garden where the praties grow.
Chorus.

    Mention of the previous number brings to mind the man who was possibly the very best performer of the simple Irish love song. Many people who had a snob mentality felt that John McCormack was letting his reputation as an international tenor down by singing such songs, but the truth is that he was able to give them a quality which very few other people could match, and he will be remembered for them long after his recordings of more pretentious works are forgotten.

      'I hear you calling me —
      You called me when the moon had veiled her light
      Before I went from you into the night. . .'

That song has an Irish flavour and it became the hallmark of McCormack. It might be well to mention, however, that it was written by an Englishman. For Sunday popular concerts in London McCormack had a fine pianist named Charles Marshall, who one day rather shyly asked whether he might bring along some of his own compositions for the singer to hear. McCormack like two of them, and Marshall was thereby encouraged to produce a third, with words by Harold Harford, which the publishers wouldn't touch. 'They say it's unsingable,' said he dolefully. 'Let's have a try,' said John. He introduced the song at the next Boosey concert, and from then on it was associated with his name.

That was in 1908.

McCormack had a passion for 'digging' as he called it, for new songs, or rather old songs which were half-remembered. One day he heard his mother-in-law humming an air which was unfamiliar. 'Where did you get that?' he asked. She described it as an old song her mother used to sing called, she thought, *The Pale Moon was Shining*. It started the tenor on a quest around the music shops of Ireland, humming what he had of the air to proprietors, until eventually he found it and as a surprise for her, sang it at a Dublin concert.

45. THE ROSE OF TRALEE

Words & Air: William Pembroke Mulchinock

THE PALE MOON WAS RIS - ING A - BOVE THE GREEN MOUN - TAIN, THE
SUN WAS DE - CLIN - ING BE - NEATH THE BLUE SEA. WHEN I STRAY'D WITH MY
LOVE TO THE PURE CRYS - TAL FOUN - TAIN, THAT STANDS IN THE BEAU - TI - FUL
VALE OF TRA - LEE. SHE WAS LOVE - LY AND FAIR AS THE ROSE OF THE
SUM - MER, YET 'TWAS NOT HER BEAU - TY A - LONE THAT WON ME, OH,
NO, 'TWAS THE TRUTH IN HER EYE EV - ER BEAM - ING, THAT MADE ME LOVE
MA - RY THE ROSE OF TRA - LEE

The cool shades of evening their mantle were spreading
And Mary all smiling was list'ning to me.
The moon thro' the valley her pale rays were shedding,
When I won the heart of The Rose of Tralee.
Though lovely and fair as the rose of the summer,
Yet 'twas not her beauty alone that won me,
Oh, no! 'twas the truth in her eye ever dawning,
That made me love Mary, The Rose of Tralee.

Mulchinock (1820-1864) wrote the song for a special purpose and person, as you may remember was the case with more than a few of the other songs. He lived near Tralee in what is now known as Clogher's House, which is on the narrow road running through Clahane just outside the town. Mary O'Connor was a servant in the house and he fell in love with her. Although of well-to-do Protestant family he supported Daniel O'Connell's Repeal movement and was in charge of a contingent of the Liberator's followers during a meeting in the town at which a man was fatally wounded. Mulchinock was held responsible and had to flee the country. He returned in 1849, through the good offices of an influential friend of the family, but by then Mary had contracted consumption and died. He is said to have written the song at that time. He later married, but unhappily. He wrote for a number of periodicals, including *The Nation* under the signatures 'W.P.M.', 'M', and 'Heremon'. There is a monument to Mulchinock and his 'Rose' in the town park of Tralee. McCormack made the song world-famous through its use in his film *Song of my Heart*.

Many of the songs in this book received magnificent treatment from McCormack: *The Dawning of the Day* and Lady Dufferin's two songs come to mind, as do many of Moore's. No one could interpret a song better. He gave every word its proper meaning and could bring even an indifferent song to life. One should say that rather than decry him for singing simple Irish songs, that they were worthy of his very special voice.

People used to say of Sir Arthur Sullivan (whose grandfather also came from Tralee, not quarter of a mile from Mulchinock's house) that he was bastardising his talent in writing comic operas with Gilbert—well, we could also say that, like McCormack, he did what he did best and did it superbly. Mention of Gilbert and Sullivan leads me to remind you of a curio—an Irish song written by W. S. Gilbert, that most English of Englishmen! He wrote the words and John L. Molloy (who gave us *Bantry Bay* and *The Kerry Dances*) wrote the music. It cannot be truly regarded as a love song of us Irish, but since it is a curio, I give an excerpt.

46. THADY O'FLYNN

Words: W. S. Gilbert
Air: J. L. Molloy

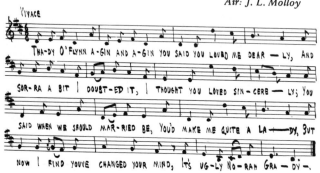

The fashion of people who were not themselves Irish writing successful songs about us and having them, in some cases, accepted as our own was undoubtedly advanced by the flood of Irish people emigrating to America. Song pluggers of Broadway soon discovered that a sentimental tune about the Emerald Isle could bring a tear to Irish eyes, and so we have such pieces as *When Irish Eyes are Smiling, Sweet Rosie O'Grady, My Wild Irish Rose, Little Annie Rooney* and *The Strawberry Blonde*, all of which make a nice waltz selection—many's the time when I was young and my feet could twinkle that I swung around to them as played by Pat Crowley's Band—but of course they are not Irish songs.

The Galway shawl obviously had its attractions as another song shows.

47. A SHAWL OF GALWAY GREY

Words: Patrick Hogan

ANDANTINO

Too— short the night we part-ed Too quick-ly came the day when
sil— ent brok-en heart-ed I.— went from you a-way The
dawn was bright'ning o'er Glen-rue As stole the stars a-way The
last fond look I caught of you in your shawl of Gal-way grey—.

Oh, I've seen the silks and laces,
 And well they look an' show.
Beneath the pretty faces
 Of gentle girls I know.
But this — a secret I'll confide —
 I'd leave them all today,
To meet you on a green hillside
 In your shawl of Galway Grey.

The well is sparkling as of yore,
 The sky still grey and blue,
The dog outside your father's door
 Keeps watch and ward for you.
And all this picture now I see,
 But, ah! so far away —
Is brightened by your grace so free
 And your shawl of Galway Grey.

Let others love some prouder dame
 With frills and flowers bedecked.

Your power o'er me is still the same,
    Its play remains unchecked.
And all I wish is for Glenrue,
    My homeland far away.
And life and love beside you
    In your shawl of Galway Grey.

So we are coming to modern times, for Padraic Colum died but recently. His tender song, written to an old air, was written many years before his death, but it should be remembered, and sung, long after his time.

48. SHE MOVED THROUGH THE FAIR

Words: Padraic Colum
Air: Traditional

She went away from me, and went through the fair,
And finally I watched her, move here and move there,
Then she went homeward with one star awake —
As the swan in the evening moves over the lake.

The people were saying no two were e'er wed,
But one had a sorrow that never was said,
She went away from me with her goods and her gear,
And that was the last that I saw of my dear.

Last night she came to me, my dear love came in,
So softly she came that her feet made no din,
She laid her hand on me, and this she did say:
'It will not be long, love, 'till our wedding day.'

Colum would appear to have fashioned his beautiful lyric on
an older ballad called *I once had a Sweetheart*, which is a
little more earthy.

This is one of the few cases where the now, more
scholarly edition could be considered better than the old.

And last of all let us show that the tradition of writing
Irish love songs has not died; and that it is still with us in
the spirit of a man who has been my friend, and whose
name appears in a dedication at the start of this book. John
B. Keane, of Listowel, who gave us *Sive* and so many other
plays; and a fine song from his play *Many Young Men of
Twenty*, in which he created the wonderful part of Danger
Mullally for me.

49. KEELTY

Words & Air: John B. Keane

I'll be waiting for you where the small waters flow,
Down here in Keelty where the whitethorns grow
The white fires of joy in your bosom will glow
When you see your fine young son down here in Keelty.

I'll be waiting for you where the cockerel cries,
Down here in Keelty where the heart in me dies:
I'll be waiting for you where the heart in me dies,
For the strength and love of you down here in Keelty.

And as we started this book with translations from original
Irish lyrics it would seem fitting to end it with the reverse
process; so here is a verse of *Keelty* written by John B.
specially for me.

A chomharsain crua-croidthe nách trua é mo sceál
Tá mo leannán caol áluinn tabhairt aghaidh ar an saol
Tá mo leannán caol áluinn imtheacht thar a'tinn
'S ní fheiceam go deó, go deó á thíos i gCaoilte.

Songs remembered; others half-forgot
—the songs of my book
bring a memory to me of times and people, past.
Maybe your own favourite has been omitted, but, in truth,
more have been written than I,
or any collector, could fit into one book.

Oft, in the stilly night,
    Ere slumber's chain has bound me.
Fond memory brings the light,
Of other days around me.